The Circus, Remembered

The circus here is as it looked, long ago, to a small English boy named Brian Wildsmith. This is a circus remembered—its clowns and tigers and acrobats summoned forth as they glowed in the mind of a certain child.

For him, the parade before the circus was an unending prelude, stretching farther than one could count or imagine. Perhaps for someone else who saw the same parade there were fewer marchers and more riders, or the other way around. But this is Brian Wildsmith's circus, and this is how he remembers it.

A delight for him were the exaggerations—the impossible things, like the six-legged horse or the slack-wire performers, moving along on a penny-farthing bicycle. Or he saw the tumblers standing in a great line, holding aloft another line, arms interlocked, with more and more tumblers on their shoulders, and more on top of those, until the whole fantastic wall of tumblers cannot be believed. But Brian Wildsmith saw it, and here it is!

He remembered other things, too—the impossibly long legs of the clowns on stilts, the jugglers doing tricks with crockery, the rising of the dappled horses to plumed heights, the simplicity of the dogs and parrots doing their tricks.

The child Brian has grown into the artist Wildsmith, and for the children everywhere, as for his own children, he has put on paper the circus marvels he recalls.

Brian
Wildsmith's

CIRCUS

Brian Wildsmith's

watts
INTERNATIONAL

CIRCUS

FRANKLIN WATTS, INC.,
845 THIRD AVENUE
NEW YORK, N.Y. 10022

© Brian Wildsmith 1970

First published 1970 by Oxford University Press
First American publication 1970 by Franklin Watts, Inc.

Library of Congress Catalog Card Number: 71-102917

SBN 531 01541 6
3 4 5 6 7 8

The circus comes to town . . .

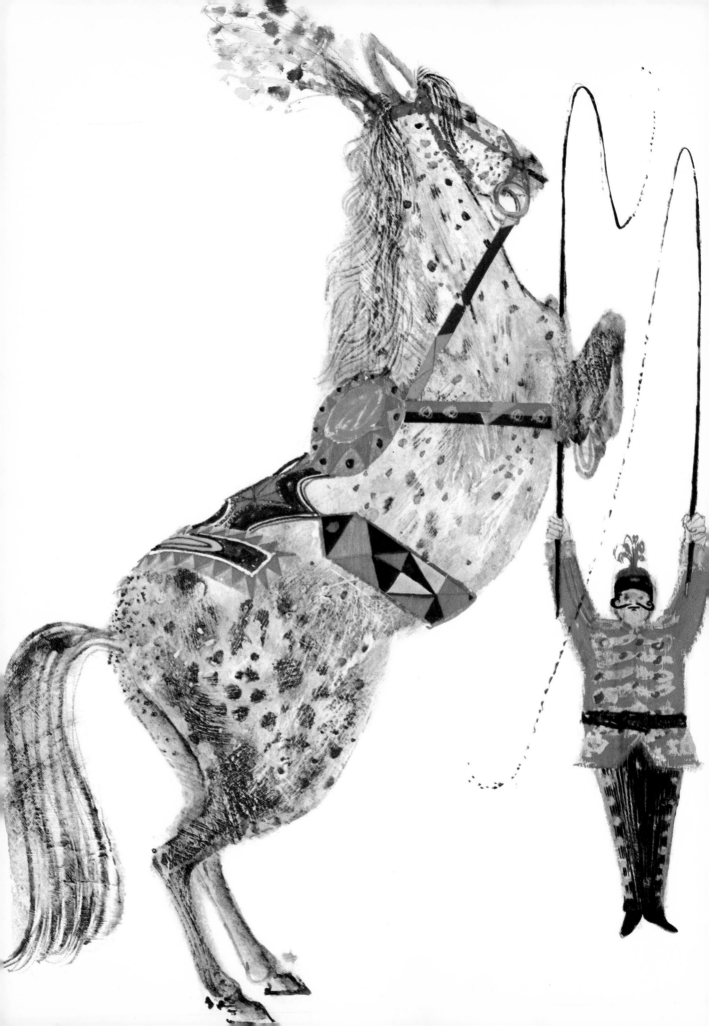

...the circus goes on to the next town.